INFORMING THE OBJECT

GUY COMELY

perspective of road entrance to
festival table

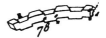

THEMES V

INFORMING THE OBJECT
Projects from Diploma Unit 1 1981-85
Unit Master Peter Wilson

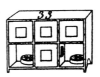

ARCHITECTURAL ASSOCIATION

THEMES V Informing the Object and the accompanying exhibition have been organised at the Architectural Association, London, through the office of the Chairman, Alvin Boyarsky, assisted by Micki Hawkes. This publication has been designed by Peter Wilson and produced through the Communications Unit, co-ordinated by Dennis Crompton, with Paul Barnett, Lisbet Kjaer, Dominique Murray, Rob Polley, Sue Rowe-Leete, Annelies Siero, Marilyn Sparrow and Gail Tandy. Production editor Vicky Wilson. Exhibition mounted by Colleen Haley. Printed in London by E G Bond Ltd. Cover silk-screened by G & B Arts Ltd.

CONTENTS

FOREWORD Alvin Boyarsky   **6**

QUOTES, AND NOTES, FROM A CONVERSATION WITH PETER WILSON Michael Gold   **7**

INTRODUCTION Peter Wilson   **11**

Dialogue 1: **APPROPRIATION AND DENSIFICATION**   **12**

Dialogue 2: **FIGURATIVE AND TECTONIC**   **17**

Dialogue 3: **PERSPECTIVE AND LANDSCAPE**   **22**

UNIT PROGRAMMES   **26**

UNIT MEMBERS   **30**

PROJECTS   **33**

CORNEL NAF Spider House   **34**

WILLIAM FIREBRACE Column/Columnist/House   **40**

WILLIAM FIREBRACE Press Archives   **42**

HIDEHIKO ASANO Light House/Dark Villa   **44**

HIDEHIKO ASANO Border Crossing   **46**

HENRY ALDRIDGE Column/Columnist/House   **50**

NEIL PORTER BBC Headquarters – An Image for Sound   **52**

GUY COMELY Langan's Restaurant   **56**

RICHARD LUNDQUIST Langan's Restaurant   **60**

RICHARD LUNDQUIST Blackfriars Bridge   **62**

BAN SHUBBER Clandeboye Arts Institute   **64**

BAN SHUBBER Calais Hypermarket   **66**

MICHAEL SEROFF Typology of the Hut   **68**

MARTYN WILTSHIRE Bridge 409   **72**

LOUIS RICO GOODWIN The BBC   **76**

KATRIN LAHUSEN Blue Bridge   **78**

BAN SHUBBER Bridge Asylum   **79**

FOREWORD

This publication is the fifth in the *Themes* series which began in 1982, designed to document aspects of the work of the Diploma School (years four and five) at the Architectural Association School of Architecture.

As has been previously stated, the intensity and the cohesiveness of the work shown here is one characteristic of the unit system which has been the basic organisational device within the school for the past thirteen years, whereby staff and students arrange themselves in self-selecting groups respecting differences in pedagogical technique, theoretical and ideological positions and attitudes towards design and style. Over the years, and particularly in the Diploma School, space has been found for long-term experiments and research involving a continuity of work, the evolution of ideas and the slow, painful emergence of confidence and a sense of style. The spirit and variety of the work produced in this way has enriched the school as a whole due to the energy and integrity of both staff and students involved in the process as demonstrated, for example, in the following pages.

By providing a statement of intentions, a précis of the programmes issued and a selection of student responses, Peter Wilson has demonstrated the continued viability of the open-ended, self-programming studio activities so characteristic of architectural education at its best. It is hoped that *Informing the Object* will be as useful and inspiring to teachers and students of architecture as the previous volumes, which include *Architecture and Continuity* (Dalibor Vesely, 1982); *Spirit and Invention* (Peter Cook and Ron Herron, 1982); *The Discourse of Events* (Bernard Tschumi, 1983); *People In Architecture* (Michael Gold, 1983).

Peter Wilson, who was associated with Leo Krier, Rem Koolhaas & Elia Zenghelis, Michael Gold and Bernard Tschumi during his student and early teaching days, represents a second generation who have extended extant propositions and experiments to a new level of resolution. Others similarly involved in teaching activities at the Architectural Association include Mohsen Mostafavi, Christine Hawley, Nigel Coates, Zaha Hadid, Peter Salter, Jeanne Sillett and Chris Macdonald, and it is hoped that future volumes in the *Themes* series will provide evidence of a continued vitality.

Alvin Boyarsky
Chairman

MICHAEL GOLD

QUOTES, AND NOTES, FROM A CONVERSATION WITH PETER WILSON

'He, like the flâneur in the city, entrusted himself to chance as a guide on his intellectual journeys of exploration.'
On Walter Benjamin
Hannah Arendt

As much as Unit 1 products – these disarticulated dogs, strings, boats, tendons, animated institutes and retreats, startled joints and precarious structures – may stir up enquiry (What is this shipshape? Is it a bird, is it a plane?); there is again as much interest to be found in Peter Wilson's teaching methods themselves, and their effect on the sensibilities of those who experience them.

'The German word *Lebenswerk*... translates as something like "life's work". It's about life and art as all rolled into one.'

Clues as to how he communicates in teaching are found in his prolific production of architectural texts in the form of written programmes, but before dealing with these, I'd like to go back to a lecture he gave in 1976 at the London Architecture Club.

Peter, at this time, had an incredible stammer. What others might regard as a problem, he, typically, turned to effect as part of his performance.

The event was set up as one of those elaborate plots, in which everything from the food to how and where everyone was to sit was brought into play.

Peter showed slides of what looked like a series of archaeological digs, with bones, artefacts, skulls, pottery shards, architectural objects, and surveyors' rods lying in hollows in the ground. A closer look also revealed things like old plastic sandals, rusty springs and kettles among the relics. A simple interpretation of these fascinating and suggestive tableaux was not possible, since objects and periods, ages and types of artefact were mixed up, and it would be hard to decide what had been there and for how long.

As Peter slowly stammered out the words, an interesting brown smear would gradually spread across the already complex image on the screen, as we waited patiently for the sentences to coalesce and the next slide to be put on to be similarly affected by the heat from the projector lamp.

As I remember it, the subject of the text was how enigmatic images can liberate the imagination, and elicit a thousand different thoughts in a thousand different heads, whereas description and interpretation tend to narrow thought, encourage conformity, and cause censorship of the possible.

Later at the Club, a set of chosen experts and others, mere artists, were asked to comment on the meaning of some famous archaeological and architectural relics. This occasion ended with arguments between the experts – belligerently determined to stick to their differing interpretations of the meaning of Stonehenge – while the artists blithely declared that everyone could be right, and added further interpretations of their own off the top of their heads.

To return to the present, and Peter's teaching at the AA. Operations begin annually with his production of a comprehensive prospectus, which reads like a curriculum for an autonomous school in miniature, a self-sufficient collage exploring the information-bit limits of the printed page, and a kind of satirical architectural broadsheet.

Where others clothe programmes with definitions of purpose, doctrinal preambles, authoritative references, or exacting accommodation schedules, Peter delivers instead a patently subjective and open-ended dissertation in the form of an arbitrary plot.

This plot usually concerns a subject, not in itself architectural, but picked seemingly at random from nature (GLASS, WATER, RUST) or from the foibles of human conduct (FAST FOOD, TRAVEL, THE PRESS). The subject is then developed via interconnected narratives, aphorisms, and images, towards the instantaneous generation of an as yet unheard of series of potential building types and forms.

'Yes, chance plays a part. One introduces a subject, not knowing precisely where it will lead . . . because one is interested in architecture as narrative – exploring purposes and having something to say apart from about its own formal composition.'

These documents exude a peculiarly elating confidence in the proposition that authentic architectural experience, and the creation of an authentic architecture, can begin anywhere, travel freely, and always lead somewhere of value, depending only on an attentive eye, a disciplined hand, and the ability to discriminate between that which is capable of being properly expressed in architectural terms, and that which isn't.

'One sets up that structure, but the effect is a tangential thing. Each goes off in their own direction . . .'

As in Dada and Surrealism, puns, alliterations, image double-entendres, are prominent, both as commentary and as techniques for developing intuition towards invention appropriate to a context. The buildings that ensue, even competition entries for large urban complexes, often run a fine line between pure architectural humour and workable proposals for the given context.

A nice pun appears in the series 'Recipes for Architecture'. In a discussion of fast food and cafés, reference is made to 'The Presence of the Pasta', and to spaghetti . . .

'Marinetti invented what was called "Futurist Cooking", consisting of recipes for salami cooked in black coffee . . . indicating the juxtapositions in the modern world, like cars and trains with cities and zoos. He wanted to do away with pasta – stodgy stuff, symbolising old ways. There was a long debate in the newspapers with the Bishop of Naples. The Bishop apparently swore on his deathbed that the angels in heaven only ate pasta . . . tagliatelle and spaghetti à la Neapolitana.'

'The Presence of the Past' had been the theme of the 1982 Venice Biennale architecture section, where much ponderous debate had been generated on 'the return of History'. Unfortunately most of the work on show had interpreted this as the return of rather flat quotes and references to architectural histories, rather than as the return of consciousness about the world at large and its potential for architectural interpretation.

'Remythologising follows on the crisis in culture – thinking of the world as quantifiable has stripped objects of their mythical capacity. As at Loos's time, mythical illusions in mass-produced decoration and reproduced style is a sham myth. It doesn't allude to anything of meaning. That was the end of a period of meaning that . . . wasn't. The Modern Movement was the washing out; then there's re-investing the world with this missing dimension. Painting today is attempting this. But what many architects are doing is repeating exactly what Loos was against. You don't find meaning in a left luggage locker. . .'

What follows from a Wilson programme, and its dense tapestry of incentives to exploration – the visits (FOOD leads to Hamburgers leads to Hamburg, WATER leads to Bath . . .

'. . . all roads don't lead to Rome)'

. . . the events, meetings in strange places, intricate technical studies in materials and original ways of drawing, I know only these days from hearsay.

'We went to Vienna when we were doing the "Press" subject. We went especially when it was the middle of winter – when you have to look at newspapers in cafés. Unfortunately very few students read German – but we acted out the ritual. But then, other things take over – accidental things. For example, finding oneself in a lot of cafés. We went to the Loos café – not the Kärtner Bar, the other one, the Café "Nihilismus" – the Café-Museum. We found out Loos used to sit there when he was very old. Loos (he was deaf) would be surrounded by his acolytes saying "Ach Meister, du bist der grösste Meister in der Welt", something like that – and he'd be cupping his hand to his ear and saying "Was? Was?". He couldn't hear a word. For someone who wrote a book called *Spoken into the Void* this is really rather poignant, ironic. Yes, it's really quite tragic, isn't it?'

'In early work one placed far more emphasis on intuition, or expression. I find I now spend far more time on the craft – on the making of things – because unless one has the technique, it is not possible to articulate the intuitions. That's why each year we do the perspective workshop, which is purely about graphic technique. Maybe perspective is a whole subject; image runs through a lot of the projects . . .'

'The other thing about intuition: it's often at the AA taken as an alternative to being literate – to be working entirely in one's own world. This is quite incorrect, working intuitively is to make unexpected or new connections between precedents. The more one knows, the more territory one has to move around in, and therefore the richer the work.'

I know more surely of the liberating effect of similar projects from a period before that dealt with in this book, when Peter, Jeanne Sillett, Paul Shepheard and I worked together as the 'Old Unit 5'.

Four tutors, and a lot of students, all then became caught up in a web of expanding connections, transfers, and fusions. Programmes became projects, projects became programmes, tutors became students, everyone including students began publishing programmes, as comment and as artworks, whenever they felt like it, which became often. I am still working through ideas that arose then, and I am sure that whatever developments have since taken place in Peter's own adventures in the art, his particular knack of releasing in others an expanded perception of the possible and the desirable, and of inspiring immense and multi-faceted craft in its pursuit, remains.

BAN SHUBBER
art school in striped landscape

INTRODUCTION   **PETER WILSON**

This publication documents four years of teaching, four years of formulating and making architecture. The following dialogues identify the essential subjects which locate this particular research both within the Architectural Association school and in a wider cultural context. But the projects are not just illustrations of a theoretical position: to them is to be added that other essential ingredient, the individual character of each student as projected and developed in their designs.

The character of the Unit itself has evolved from and been informed by other experiences within the AA. From 1979 to 1980 Jenny Lowe and myself as the then Intermediate Unit 1 rehearsed many of the current themes. Prior to that Mike Gold, Jeanne Sillett, Paul Shepheard and myself taught as Diploma Unit 5 and even prior to that were essential years as student with and then assistant to Elia Zenghelis. This propagation of influence and attitude is now extending in the opposite direction as Diploma Unit 1 graduates teach another generation of students. Hopefully they too will be infected with that dimension of architecture which makes dream-like connections real and which transports us with optimism and delight in our inventions.

DIALOGUE 1:
APPROPRIATION AND DENSIFICATION

Within the work of the Unit a consistent and not entirely conventional approach to 'the problem of the city' has been developing. The starting point for each exercise has provided a framework for this emerging theory, but it is the repeated explorations of individual students that have produced the inventions, refinements and truly original moves.

While glancing sideways at contemporary urban theory, our interest has remained inclusivist and undoctrinaire. Early Press Projects like Mike Wolfson's square surrounded by newspaper and archive slabs used a contemporary language of abstract wall and localised articulations to frame a space fundamentally differentiated from its surrounding fabric. Similarly but in the inverse Ban Shubber created an internalised fortress for the island site of the BBC headquarters. Such strong-arm insertions are intentional shock therapy for the city. On the other hand it was not form but a

12

MICHAEL WOLFSON

press archive/press square

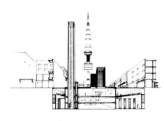

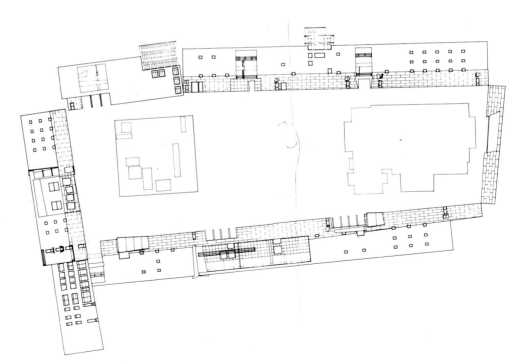

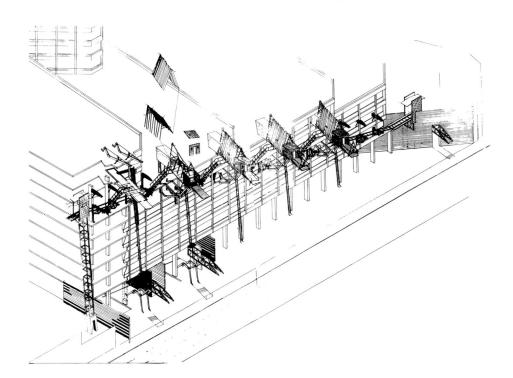

COSTAS DAVARIS

marginal parasites

EMI office block

choreography of movement which generated Neil Porter's BBC headquarters project. The building – an inverted model of the city itself – needs its roof (hat) to reassert the unity of a block otherwise transgressed from all sides.

The programme for the BBC headquarters, a large and complex institution occupying a territory somewhere between building and block, precipitated a spectrum of strategies. Significantly the project of L.R. Goodwin, although apparently abstract to the point of transparency, provided a prescription for an extreme spatial and material sensuality. The implied infinite reverberation of sound, delineated by focusing the sound in a forest of speaker columns, transformed an ostensibly dry programme into a precise and sensual spatial experience.

By accepting existing infrastructure, together with the fact that massive expansion or remaking of cities is both unachievable and unacceptable, we have come by default to the hypothesis of localised if fundamental readjustment. Selective insertion of architectural provocateurs has been pursued as an appropriate contemporary mode of action at the scale of the city (densification) and of the individual building (appropriation). At both scales the intended consequence is both remedial and generative of new uses and meanings.

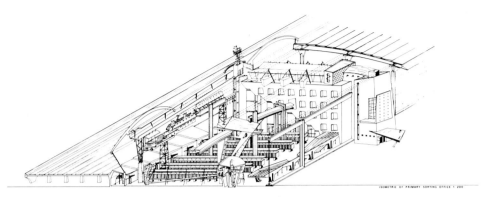

ISOMETRIC OF PRIMARY SORTING OFFICE 1 200

KATARZYNA PIOTROWSKA

all-night post office/night club
dormitories for nocturnals, new
covent garden

urban scale straddle building; the
railway at new covent garden
spanned by this stage/table for
urban spectaculars, housing and
float hangers

GUY COMELY

14

DISTRICT DENSIFICATION. Two quarters of London have been studied and used as vehicles for densification. The intention has been to accept the given matrix, and then to identify and extrapolate the latent and unique character of the place as the generator of a series of often contradictory interventions.

In the case of the heavily built-up Fleet Street area – characterised by the production of words and newspapers – it became necessary first to demarcate the zone in question. Its perimeter was materialised into a series of contemporary 'barriers'. The figurative Columnists' Houses which resulted were contextually parasitic, local intensifications occupying blank walls, traffic islands and any other subversive wedges available between public and private territory. Subsequent Press Projects continued this overlaying of the area with the juxtaposition of public and private properties, again a prerequisite for the Press Archives and for the 'Bridge of Villas each with Station of Service'.

In the case of the Fruit and Vegetable Market at Nine Elms, the problem was the re-urbanisation of a functional archipelago, and its reconnection with the River Thames. Character was extrapolated from found conditions; food was the subject. The surrounding landscape of truck-park generated a territorial surface never entirely to be filled.

The accumulation of new layers at Nine Elms began with a scattering of instant archaeology – pavilions for growers and sellers, tide measurement and other found attributes of the site. Two organising strategies emerged – a series of routes from market to river and a pattern of vegetable garden textures repeating the dimensions of the market sheds. Each student evolved particular modes of occupation at these different scales. The final assemblage, a common model, mixed the specificity of careful design with found fabric represented by the original subject of food (spaghetti for railways, sugar-cube terraces and macaroni forests).

bridge museum plan

bridge museum section

LOCAL APPROPRIATION. Pursuing the insertion of vagabond architecture at a small scale, two rooftop sites for Langan's Restaurant were chosen. This promoted a radical recoding of already dense contexts. The roof of the Economist Building prompted refined technical resolutions from Richard Lundquist while Clinton Terry demonstrated an unexpected transformational delicacy, employing steel adjacencies to the concrete frames. The alternative rooftop – an electrical substation – required figurative as well as structural invention. Guy Comely's restaurant-as-horse appropriated not only the site but also a predominant position on the London skyline.

For the Chip Facade project on Tottenham Court Road, a strategy to restructure less than adequate office facades was developed. Marginal living and the reformation of an urbanised street were the by-products. At a slightly larger scale, the stranded left-over columns of the abandoned nineteenth-century Blackfriars bridge, which used to span the River Thames, were the subject of appropriation. Varying degrees of physical intervention seemed possible. Katrin Lahusen juggled with toy-like objects and one principal screen element. Martyn Wiltshire did much more by connecting to Blackfriars station and visually tying into larger urban networks. He proposed station towers and a new Southbank Institute of Contemporary Furniture.

Finally, perhaps the most subtle urban appropriation is the movable building. Michael Seroff's huts, originally designed for the Tottenham Court Road Chip Facade, contained in their mobility the threat of appearing overnight in Trafalgar Square or against any inadequate facade. Institutionalising this family of subversive architecture, he went on to design the Blackfriars site as Art Hut Factory.

These projects suggest that the making and occupation of architecture is a public and cultural ritual and that truly urban architecture consists in small, highly charged and city-changing interventions.

15

blackfriars pre-columbian museum – figurative appropriation of site, an autonomous urban element

ANDREW KAMINS

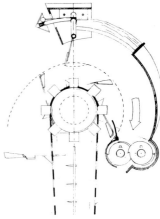

souvenir destroyer

a domestic object for the sorting of
souvenirs, shelves agitated by
ticklers shuffle objects downwards

only objects regularly rescued avoid
the crusher

spring-powered animation by fruit
machine handle

tectonic figure

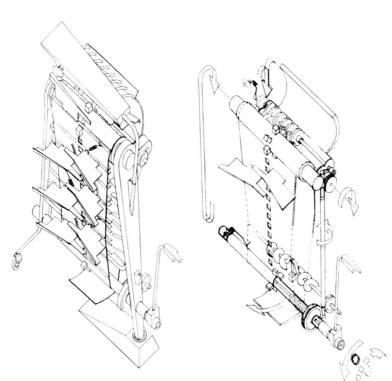

NEIL PORTER

Two concepts have emerged as essential to Diploma 1 strategy: the figurative and the tectonic. The first is the capacity of architecture to project multiple and poetic experience, the second the promotion of a physical specificity. The subsequent overlaying of these two fields of research has predictably led to a tectonically refined figuration, the concept informing the object.

Over and above the requirements of use and stability, there is the necessity for buildings to be informed by subjects, dialogues and narratives that connect them to a wider sphere of knowledge and experience. Figuration is the mode of formation of this rhetorical dimension.

METAPHORIC FIGURATION. From the outset a metaphoric figuration has informed projects like Hidehiko Asano's Light House/Dark Villa. Here an ostensibly pragmatic programme of a villa on a disused railway viaduct is transformed into a terrifying poetic, first by the informing narrative and then by the invention of an equivalent material dimension. It is an asylum, a precise mechanism for the treatment of its single occupant, an autistic child. From the Light House a beam ruptures both architectonic and symbolic layers of the house to reach the subject quite literally held at its centre. Like the work of de Sade or Mishima this project tests moral preconceptions. The figuration has a precise communicative role. The Dark Villa is closer to Lequeu than to Boullée. Like Lequeu's, the contemporary sensibility is troubled, a synthesis of discontinuous quotes, both sophisticated and naive in composition and rendering.

CORPORAL FIGURES. Stressing the corporal integrity and internal consistency of a particular element requires the identification and exaggeration of its character. With the programme for the Columnists' Houses, located on the pavements and leftover corners around Fleet Street, a particular local architectural personality-type was implied. William Firebrace's journalist was just such a figure, his tower's character being informed by the contrivance of an internal optical illusion – now he's at work, now he's not.

Even closer to a literal reading are the giant masks disguising Makoto Saito's Floating Red Light District or Andrew Kamins's project for Tottenham Court Road. The subversive potential of the figure is identified here. Small in scale in comparison to its context, it nevertheless exploits this difference by assuming the role of principal

17

masked towers
red light district
MAKOTO SAITO

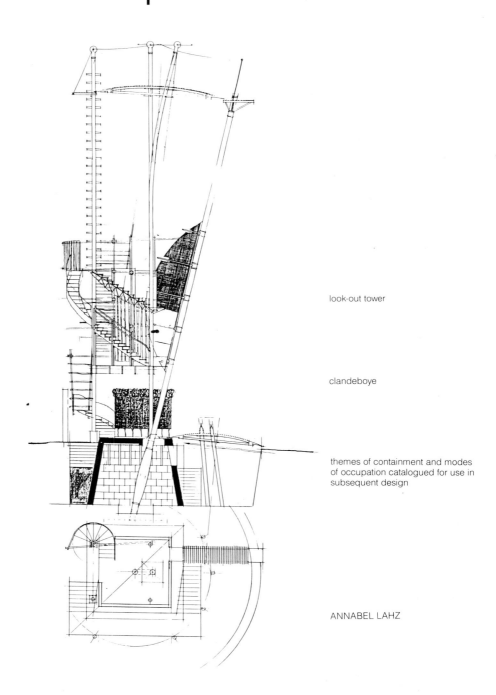

look-out tower

clandeboye

themes of containment and modes of occupation catalogued for use in subsequent design

ANNABEL LAHZ

performer, thus relegating its ignoble context to the status of backdrop. Similarly a tower-like structure can become the register for landscape contexts. With the tectonic interpretation of found conditions – earth, hedge and treetop – as subject, the tower proposed by Annabel Lahz at Clandeboye performs this role.

Having made the association between figure and tower, it follows that an institution the size of an urban block can also be divided into its constituent family members, a crowd of towers. Katarzyna Piotrowska in her BBC headquarters project did just that. Similarly Andrew Kamins's Blackfriars bridge established its horizontal self-containment in a series of transformations from the original metaphor, an Indian painting of a sleeping animal.

FIGURATIVE SUBJECTS – PRESS, TRAVEL, FOOD. Since 1981 each year's programmes have been linked by a common subject tangential to the discipline of architecture. From this common starting point students have developed individual preoccupations and interpretations. The recurrent subject provides a field of spatial and programmatic research, and figurative incentives.

The first subject was the Press. This used a ready-made site, Fleet Street, and provided building types like the Columnists' Houses and Press Archives.

As summary descriptions of both site and subject, William Firebrace used nine standard headlines – 'African Coup', 'Pet Rescue', etc. – to generate two descriptive buildings. Paired across Fleet Street, each has a plan of nine equal squares, with the differences between the two developed as contrasting press interpretations. The wit of such analysis survives the trap of illustration by overlaying this highly charged dimension with a more prosaic credibility of use.

Travel as subject gave us figurative topics like the 'Iconography of Ships', 'Codes of Border Crossing' and the 'Domestic Status of Souvenirs'. Next the catalyst was Food, as in Marinetti's Futurist Cooking (a polemic against the presence of the pasta). Production, distribution and consumption of food, like architecture, are fundamental activities, and, like architecture, they become both rationalised and ritualised.

FIGURATIVE MOVES AND MOVING FIGURES. Using the metaphor of the fashion journalist as spider trapping her victims in webs of appearance, Cornel Naf developed from the initial Press subject not only a figurative language but also a self-informing process of design. This subjective evolution is a process of continual generation and mutation. At first the interviewer of great Italian designers is literally the spider. Web-like drawings of her house include a vocabulary of wooden screens,

street figure

ANDREW KAMINS

19

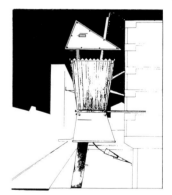

BBC crowd

KATARZYNA PIOTROWSKA

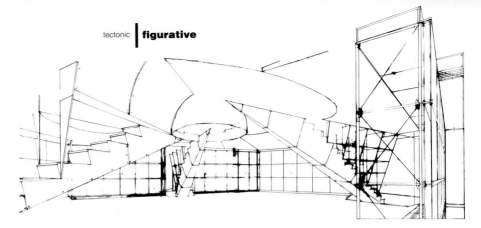

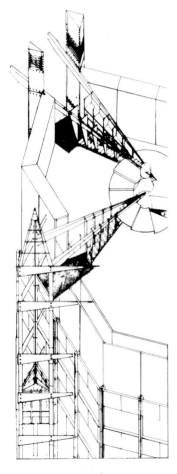

aesthetic insulation to isolate the hunting ground, food bags and typewriter – all in a state of decomposition. Next the subject becomes architectural fashion, specifically Libera's Villa Malaparte. More elements of the vocabulary emerge as this also is decomposed until finally the process synthesises into its final form, the Fashion Institute, a monumental artificial island located, like the Villa Malaparte, on Capri, the playground of its subjects, Armani, Versaci, etc. One would expect the metaphor to end with the illustration of this bizarre programme, but its true provocation lies in the subsequent deadpan technical drawings. Here the specificity of boat hoists, marble floors and air-conditioning vents is prescribed in careful detail, always motivated by and extending the figurative subject. Sensual and figurative tectonics like this and later projects obviously contain a very different sensibility to that branch of architecture generated by technological procedures.

Rather than design moves, Neil Porter's Souvenir Sorting Machine takes movement within the object itself as its subject. The machine is a travel-generated artefact, a domestic automaton. Clockwork vibrators shuffle its objects along shelves towards a crusher from which they must regularly be rescued. Again the mechanistic specificity gives the poetic a material credibility.

This interest in refined physicality is seen in the increasing use of models as precise objects to accompany the evocation of drawings. In his pavilion models for the Nine Elms Fruit and Vegetable Market, Richard Lundquist is also motivated by movement. The House to be Entered by Somersaulting and the Rooftop Boat House identify the essential difference between the actual movement of the occupant and the implied movement of the architecture.

MATERIAL AND THE TECTONIC. The themes of the last two years have focused on material qualities superimposed on the familiar method of subject development. Wood, steel and stone, the sources for elemental perception, are now

CLINTON TERRY

langan's restaurant

articulated through the figurative process. Extracts from the captions to Richard Lundquist's drawings demonstrate this sensibility: '…the bedroom, two plywood discs with stretched leather walls …the bath enclosed in two walls of leaves pressed between plate glass…' His later models for Langan's Restaurant and Blackfriars bridge refine this precise and yet archaic language. The juxtaposition of taut skins, steel masts, wooden ribs and the occasional unexpected anatomical junction becomes even more evocative by being set in familiar urban situations.

The myth of the primitive hut as a mammoth's ribcage may be interpreted as a reference for this work, a part of our collective subconscious. If so, it can also be read into the figurative structures of Guy Comely. His Langan's Restaurant is derived from the owner sketched as a rider astride his restaurant/horse. This figurative image suggested that the principal building frame should be hung from its structural backbone and held up by animal-like leg structures. The retreat for the principal figure, a little wooden house, is firmly in the saddle. A highly original language is pursued both at the scale of the site and at the level of interior detail.

Similar inventions, architectural accompaniments to eating, are to be found in other schemes. For Martyn Wiltshire the active element is a giant movable door that divides the two halves of his Clandeboye dining shed. For Clinton Terry it is the seige tower lifts that permit and describe the appropriation of his rooftop site.

Our current interest in the tectonic – the study of architecture not as abstract manipulations but as material assemblage – is dependant on the preceding figurative researches. The term 'tectonic' is intended to distinguish our interest in informed detail from that of technical complexity for its own sake. For example, Ban Shubber in her design for the Clandeboye landscape defines her subject as an inverted bridge to be occupied troll-like in thin glass piers. Although such a starting point is intuitive, a reaction to site and an invention of subject, its subsequent pursuit is logical and rigorous. The conclusion is a highly resolved and highly original artefact, a tectonic conspiracy of wood, steel and glass.

RICHARD LUNDQUIST

clandeboye carrel

clandeboye library

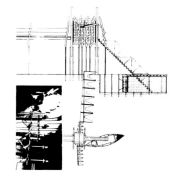

NEIL PORTER

hypermarket

composite perspective

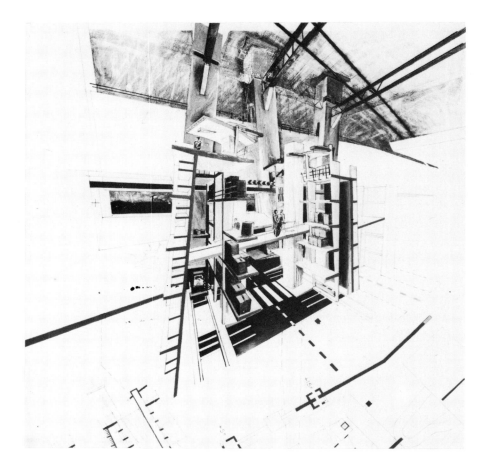

22

DIALOGUE 3:

PERSPECTIVE AND LANDSCAPE

Outside the influences of subject and context, two other essential horizons recur as data for the Unit's work – perspective and landscape.

THE PERSPECTIVE WORKSHOP. This ten-day studio exercise has been an essential input in each year's structure. For the last three years it has been run by Neil Porter, himself a student in the first workshop. The didactic purpose of the workshop lies in the protracted and apprentice-like necessity to produce the labour-intensive drawings. The setting-up of complex projections is the craft through which a truly three-dimensional perception is developed, a struggle quite different from spirited scribble.

The horizon line itself in a carefully set-up perspective, repeatedly bisected by a jungle of hieroglyphic calibrations, is witness to these painstaking lessons. Such procedural evidence – horizons, set-up lines and tangential studies – not excluded from the final images, and its presence profoundly differentiates this type of drawing from illusory perspective.

SCOTT KEMP

clandeboye institute

CONTEMPORARY PERSPECTIVE. The acceptance as format of the two-dimensional surface of the page itself, and not the implied three-dimensional space beyond, circumvents the stalemate of nineteenth-century perspective. The intention is not the limited role of perspective as formal confirmer and controller of the perceived world.

Taking cues from Duchamp's non-visual perspective and symbolic baroque configurations has led to complex overlays of projection system, spatial illusion and sensual detail. The gap between object and mind, fundamental to the historic evolution of perspective and essential for the domination of nature by Enlightenment reason, is circumvented when the opacity of both object and system are brought into question.

Including both the set-up lines and the architecture described engenders spatial juxtapositions, added to which are the multiple projections – plans floating on floors, sections folded out – and always the threat of reassemblage. Such slidings up and down the spider's web of projection lines characterises the drawings of Guy Comely and Neil Porter, among others. The sensibility is one of discontinuity and flux, but always at the centre – rotated, penetrated, explored and refined – is the precise architectural object.

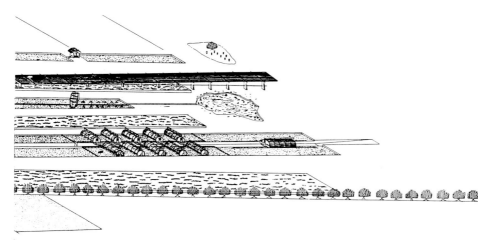

1

2

1 model farm strip layout

2 shed appropriation

3 dining shed for artists and gardeners

3

MARTYN WILTSHIRE

VIRTUAL AND PHYSICAL HORIZONS. Perspective is of course a landscape of the mind, a hypothetical construct whose emptiness extends from the eye of the viewer to the horizon – that is, until it is populated by our inventions. This is also true of the natural landscape if we imagine ours as the first interventions. Such architecture requires not only formal but also mythological invention, a ritual dimension like the brazen plough that prescribed the perimeter of Romulus's Rome. Hidehiko Asano's metaphoric Border Crossing developed from an everyday event to this level of meaning. Similarly Cornel Naf produced cliff-like buildings by an exercise in landscape negation, carving up Capri like a Cartesian cake.

Regularly our projects return to actual landscapes to clarify fundamental relationships between building, earth and sky. It is inevitable here that our insertions will not be entirely alien, they will be infected by texture and the morphology of the contours as well as by the grains of previous occupation.

Ban Shubber in her Calais Border Station devised a building that was literally an imprint of its sand dune site. Bunker-like roofs cast in the dune sand were elevated to create the building, strange, man-made mountains, which, like their surroundings, sported tufty toupées. In her later project for a Clandeboye Arts Institute she found a new natural order for a site heavily polluted with rubbish. Parallel lines of like material – steel, plastic, stone, etc. – were ordered carpet-like across the site to create a

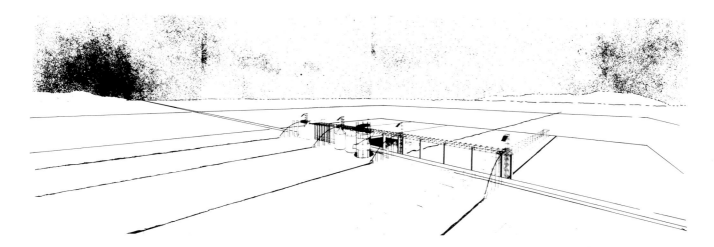

MATTHEW MISZEWSKI

purification plant in an arid
landscape (1986)

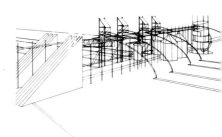

new archaeological grain oblivious of contours. It is one of these lines that eventually evolves into a linear sequence of buildings.

Other Clandeboye schemes took their cue from the found vernacular language. Working in this genre, Martyn Wiltshire began by studying hay sheds and by occupying them with provocative infills. From this experience he developed the massive 'Rural Roof' building type, a long house for artists and gardeners. Richard Lundquist on the other hand carefully played the sophisticated against the primitive. His contemporary extension to the stately home is to be read both as a new formal garden of sculptural but architectonic elements and as a mirror which doubles the existing internal rooms – library, dining-room, etc. Subtle geometric resolutions are matched by constructive invention. Seen against stone and stucco, the new pieces are decidedly of the landscape – wooden frames, walls of leaves pressed between glass, metal rain catchers and a dining-table with built-in hearth sunk below the horizon.

Finally for the recent purification plant project, perspective and the landscape converge, each giving substance to the other. Matthew Miszewski's building, a pure and almost abstract machine drawn precisely in mechanical perspective, issues water to a landscape that is at the outset just horizon and perspectival road. Once irrigated, the landscape is predictably transformed, sprouting colour, texture and depth. When the process is complete these qualities will also have invaded the architecture.

The 'press precinct', Fleet Street and its surrounds, is a district of London synonymous with the press, a 'city within a city' perhaps. But we know from Calvino and Benjamin that cities are not only rational physical entities; they also have a potency as momentary perceptions, fragments of experience, memory and disassociated elements. The press projects attempt to engender this level of characterisation through proposed physical interventions.

Project one:
COLUMN/COLUMNIST/HOUSE
**Defining the limits of the precinct, historically the parish of St Bride's bounded by the Thames, the River Fleet and the Inns of Court, this programme proposes a series of events to demarcate the perceptual boundary, to demarcate the point of entry.
DENSIFICATION: inserting more into an already congested situation. Here we insert street architecture, pavement pavilions. Precedent: Temple Bar, an occupied gate from city to West End.
COLUMN: The precedents of the Pravda building and the Chicago Tribune link this building type with the Press. The Columnist House has this iconic function; it is also one of the few options on a postage stamp site.
COLUMNIST HOUSE: a house for one individual, an existential space with its qualities and rituals isolated and exaggerated.
SIXTEEN SITES: points of entry as given on the site map with one column to be built each year.**
Project duration: 6 weeks

Project two:
PRESS SPACE/PRESS ARCHIVE
After the perimeter, the centre: a static point in the busy passage of Fleet Street, a public event framed by the archive. Visit the archives of the British Library newspaper division at Colindale – miles of paper, indiscriminate history, memory. As the production of newspapers moves away from Fleet Street the problem becomes one of representation: the image of the press. The elusive question of architectural experience is to be considered relative to this passage from Walter Benjamin: '. . . buildings are appropriated in a twofold manner: by use and by perception, or rather by touch and by sight. Such appropriation cannot be understood in terms of the attentive concentration of a tourist in front of a famous building. On the tactile side there is no counterpoint to contemplation on the optical side. Tactile appropriation is accomplished not so much by attention as by habit. As regards architecture habit deter-

mines to a large extent even optical perception . . .' The question of habit calls into question the traditional prescription for public space, the square. The problem here is that of a contemporary public space, its mode of occupation. The device to act as frame or non-frame is the archive, its mechanics and its relation as institution to the public realm.
ACCOMMODATION: a) the public space (piazza and passage as precedent); b) the archives, one library for each paper; c) stationers, coffee house, press lobby; d) words (space to let, the standard clock, post no bills, caution steps, to the public please protect and preserve these new plantings).
Project duration: 10 weeks

Project three:
FROM THE BRIDGE OF VILLAS TO THE STATION OF SERVICE
**Extending the precinct, colonising push to the east. The disused railway viaduct and vacant site at Ludgate Hill are the site.
BRIDGE OF VILLAS: a 20x20m plot on the viaduct for an urban villa (freestanding building subdivided into a number of apartments, studios, workshops).
STATION OF SERVICE: to be located east of the viaduct, one to each villa. Edges of cities and railway arches are littered with random service points (car wash, storage, mechanics, etc.). Unlike the villas, whose sites are precise and in series, these points are random colonisations of this disused no man's land.
VIENNA TRIP: Vienna's unfamiliarity should bring into focus urban qualities and elements, ordinary as well as grand (service and villa), as well as the everyday reading of newspapers in coffee houses.**
Project duration: 8 weeks

Project four:
TO THE THAMES, THE FACE OF IT
**The proposition is for the 'press precinct' as perceived from the Thames, an urban facade that distinguishes this from any other quarter. The problem of bridging the traffic chasm of Victoria Embankment and reuniting the tissue of the city with the river is to be tackled.
PROGRAMME: a Tourist Processor, accommodation for a batallion of tourists, approximately 400. Optional – luxury suites, dormitories, coach park, lido. Press conference rooms, public loggia.
SUBJECT: the conjunction of press personnel and the press precinct with that other (itinerant) population in search of that other (ephemeral) city.**
Project duration: 7 weeks

press precinct

world and not just to architectural precedent. Literacy is then not expounded for its own sake but is necessarily developed as the structuring discipline to render these non-architectural sources coherent as architecture.

INCIDENTAL AND EXCEPTIONAL: exceptional buildings are of course cultural landmarks, we have all travelled to see them. Masked by their familiarity but with an alternative provocation are the incidental spaces one travels through – tube escalators, ticket counters, spaces of arrival, border crossings. The first programme is the conjunction of two such prosaic events: the border and the hypermarket. The habitual forms and rituals of each will obviously mutate as a consequence of their overlap.

Project one:
AWAYDAY
Day-trip to Calais (site and hypermarket). Train leaves Charing Cross 7.20am returns 10.15pm.
BORDER SITE: the building is to be located between hoverport and ferry terminal (sand dunes) at Calais. Each of these contains a customs barrier, the new building must also straddle the border line.
PROGRAMME: the building is a hypermarket, selling bulk and duty free goods.
Project duration: 8 weeks
Week 9: Perspective workshop

Project two:
SOUVENIRS (a thing given or kept in memory of a person, place or event)
As tangible memory of travel, souvenirs take their place in our domestic spaces. This project is very simple – it is to design a piece of furniture/container/frame for six souvenirs, three given, three found.
Such an object has potential in the extremes of both banality and ritual. As the first, it is neutral and the souvenirs the figurative element. As the second, memory is promoted to the realm of activity, the piece becomes a narrative response to the origins of the artefact.
DAY ONE: 11am introduction, initial recording of the three given souvenirs. 1pm British Museum Drawing, experimental drawing of given souvenirs in found situations and containers. Evening, choose and record three personal souvenirs.
DAY TWO: 10.30am jury on drawings of six souvenirs. 2pm reworking and representation, first concept of domestic object.
DAY THREE: tutorials.
DAY FOUR: 10.30am jury on finished objects. 4pm choose groups for part two – A ROOM WITH THREE SOUVENIR STATIONS

DAY FIVE: tutorials, 2pm visit.
DAY SIX: jury, domestic object and rooms.

Project three:
THE BBC (have you ever travelled to Ambridge)
Within the premise of incidental buildings one travels through and exceptional buildings one travels to see, this building must be the latter. It is for the current proposition to build a new BBC building on the Langan Hotel site opposite the existing BBC in Langham Place (radio = armchair travel).
PART ONE: The public space with four pavilions. The public space is to take into account the site influences: Regent Street, All Souls, Portland Place, etc. The pavilions are to represent Radio 1, Radio 2, Radio 3 and Radio 4. Duration 2 weeks, during which time each student will research and present one of the following topics to the unit: radio stations (Vienna etc.), the 1930s BBC building; Regent Street history; site history; masts aerials and information booths; survey team; model team.
PART TWO: detailed design – image and technique. Although the complex programmatic and operational criteria must be met, the question of the appropriate image for radio is of equal significance. Public accessibility is here a vital criterion, clues to narrative inventions may be found in foyers, public rights of way, shops, banks etc., roof amenities, aerials.
PROGRAMME: (see BBC detailed requirements)
Control room, output controlled, high security, natural light. Twelve continuity suites, live broadcasting, presentation and network. News and current affairs offices, Studio suites news and current affairs, general studios (2 large and 12 small), sport and outside broadcasting, drama studios, sound archive, offices, engineering, catering etc. (see programme for square metres).
Project duration: 12 weeks

Project four:
FAST AND SLOW HOUSE
Fast and Slow Site – typical city condition, the river embankment, the Left Bank of the Seine. Fast upper embankment (traffic, speed) and slow lower embankment (the river). Height between the two six metres. The house is for two types of traveller – fast (planes, trains, credit cards) and slow (ramble, circuitous route, agonising wait, sleep after lunch). Travel is by nature the antithesis of house occupation. This house is a starting point, a goal or, for interrupted travel, a resting point.
Project duration: 6 weeks including Paris visit

left bank site

27

The subject of travel is of course an expedient. Its purpose is the generation of otherwise inconceivable architectures that respond to the modes and manners of the prosaic

Project one:
FAST FOOD AND HUNTING (the Hamburger Choice)
Site Domplatz, Hamburg. Typically for a historically important site (the founding place of this city) with layers of memory below its surface, today Domplatz is contextually desecrated. An inconclusive space in need of a new raison d'être, an architectural and programmatic invasion, in this case with food as the subject. The first 'food' programme is obviously about invention, the two extremes of finding a meal in the title can be seen as a literal brief or as abstracted. Fast Food is the sensibility of automation, functional specificity and placelessness, at the same time it is a fruitful source of contemporary spatial and visual syntax. Hunting, on the other hand, is archaic, elemental, a source of ritual – man in direct and violent relation to his dinner.
Project duration: 3 weeks

Project two:
LANGAN'S ROOFTOP RESTAURANT
**Restaurant – a place for the consumption of food. A lobster in a laquered cubicle is not the same as a pizza in a pool overlooking New York. Architecture influences digestion.
PROGRAMME: a house with a restaurant, a restaurant with a house. Seating for 100 people, bar, washrooms, kitchen and a house/appartment for owner/proprietor/raconteur Peter Langan.
CLIENT: the exact private/public relationship will be an architectural interpretation of Langan's style of life and style of restauranting. (Meeting with Peter Langan 5.30pm 11 October.)
TWO SITES: Both sites are rooftops (densification and appropriation). The roof of the Smithsons' Economist Building and the roof of the electrical substation in Masons Yard, Mayfair. On either site the new hat must not lead directly on to the existing building (straddle).**
Project duration: 6 weeks including perspective workshop

Project three:
NEW COVENT GARDEN GARDENS
**The third food programme takes as its subject food distribution, in particular FRUIT AND VEGETABLES. This focuses attention on the New Covent Garden Market at Nine Elms. Before the moving of the market to Nine Elms in 1973 the area of Covent Garden was pervaded by and gained character from the market activities in conjunction with the normal mechanisms of a city, offices, Opera House etc. The thesis of this programme is that such a fruity mix of market and daily life is a necessary and desirable urban condition. To counteract the ghettoisation of functional zoning it is now necessary to reconnect city functions to New Covent Garden. Obviously the scale of contemporary marketing and the unique characteristics of the area (river frontage, railway viaduct) will generate unfamiliar and intense architectures.
SITE: this is an urban scale project dealing with the complex mechanisms of London from Vauxhall bridge to Battersea Power Station. It is to be considered as a quarter with 'food' as its identifying character.
STRATEGY: two weeks analysis and planning concurrent with two exercises.
Exercise One: GARDENS. As a method of conceptual appropriation, the site is to be ordered by a system of nine gardens. Each student is to design a distribution masterplan to be decided in seminar.
Exercise Two: POINTS PAVILIONS PERSONALITIES. A second overlay, a series of small objects, an instant archaeology, one by each student.
Individual Programmes: in seminar in the third week, each student will take on a part of the masterplan roughly equivalent in scale to a large mixed-use building.**
Project duration: 12 weeks including Milan trip and collage workshop (Cornel Naf)

Project four:
CLANDEBOYE ESTATE
This project has a landscape site, the zone of food production. The client is the Marchioness of Dufferin and Ava, special consultant Cedric Price. The problem is to devise new and public programmes for the Clandeboye Estate. Six particular areas are to be studied initially: the Avenue, a two mile ramble, beech/station/entrance; the Motel, Belfast Road site; Walled Garden, institute or allotments; Model Farm; House and Yards, past and future; woods, husbandry and regulated use.
Project duration: 9 weeks including Clandeboye visit

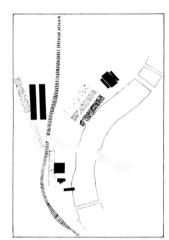

gardens

district model – food

campus, like the garden and the cemetery, is a testing ground for city models, an ideal city.
TWO SITES: a) the Lead Mines, a landscape site at the far end of the estate (isolation); b) the Walled Garden, proximity to the house.
Stage 1: Arts Lab/Botanical Studio, a focus building
Week 5: Perspective workshop
Stage 2: Institute design.
Project duration:
12 weeks including Clandeboye visit

Project two:
FACADE CHIP HOUSE CHIP SHOP
Visiting critic: Professor Lars Lerup
A six-week project to design a city facade, house and electronics bazaar. The site is the pavement, colonnade and front facade of the EMI building in Tottenham Court Road, London's silicone high street. The issues are: broken perimeter, city repairs, densification. Parasitic house, marginal living, chip shop, electronic life. The project begins with a site survey, model construction and the presentation of a proposal by each student in model form at the end of the first week. The direction each project takes will at this point be identified and persued during the weeks that follow.
Project duration: 6 weeks

Project three:
THE INHABITED BRIDGE
This project deals with both the life and the absence of life in the centre of London. Blackfriars railway bridge and the areas falling under its influence to the north and south of the river constitute the site. The spanning trusses of the original railway bridge have been removed to leave the twelve columns standing in the framed space between road and current railway bridge. In particular the tops of these columns, each with a loading capacity of 400 tons, constitute the site to be considered.
PART ONE: is to do with understanding the topology of the site; in time, high and low tide; as poetic fragments (see T S Eliot, *The Wasteland*); the potentiality of the site as inhabited bridge, Southbank Arts Stadium. Site presentation and choice of subject in week 2.
PART TWO: is the exploration of potential programmes of occupation. Found conditions, station, bridge as route, office apartment accommodation. Potential conditions: station/hotel; stadium for athletics or art; public space, event or specialist pavilion.
PART THREE: context urban scale; site limits, differentiation or coherence with existing fabric. Subjects: strategies, new elements.
Project duration: 12 weeks

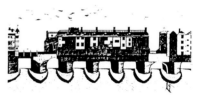

blackfriars

Project one:
THE CLANDEBOYE INSTITUTE
Following last year's small-scale interventions at the Clandeboye Estate this second stage tests the consequences of a major intervention, an Academic Institute. This stage is presumed to co-exist with the house and earlier fringe adjustments. The hypothetical model for the institute combines Fine Arts and Environmental Studies. Population 350: this number of staff and students is fixed. As the nature of the project is experimental, it is expected that the design should clarify the exact nature of the organisation. The

1981–82

1982–83

Unit Master
Peter Wilson

Unit Master
Peter Wilson

Technical Tutor
Tony McIntyre

Technical Tutor
Peter Salter

Students
Henry Aldridge
Hidehiko Asano
Sumaya Bardawil
Thomas Deckker
Graham Fairley
Andrea Fink
William Firebrace
Martin Greenland
Louis Rico Goodwin
Tim Inskip
Juha Kaapa
Lisette Khalatschi
Cornel Naf
Anthony Politis
Thomas Stankiewicz
Marjory Stave
Carolyn Trevor
Michael Wolfson

Students
Hidehiko Asano
Guy Comely
Eleni Deane
Rowena Fuller
Louis Rico Goodwin
Nigel Humphrey
Yasmin Mohamed Zain
Alvise Marsoni
Elsie Owusu
Neil Porter
Katarzyna Piotrowska
Jeremy Pitts
Zwi Rubinstein
Marjory Stave
Ban Shubber
Thomas Stankiewicz
Stephen Wright

Special thanks to:
Martin Pawley
Herman Czech
Barbara Wace
Fan Lenroc

Special thanks to:
Peter Davidson
David Chipperfield

1983–84

Unit Master
Peter Wilson

Technical Tutor
John Adden

Tutor
Neil Porter

Guest Tutor
Cornel Naf

Students
Guy Comely
Clinton Terry
Katarzyna Piotrowska
Byron Carlson
Dominic Cullinan
Rowena Fuller
Peter Möller
William Mount
Zwi Rubinstein
Makoto Saito
Tony Sharplanin
Solomon Soong
Sejal Patel
Richard Lundquist
Jean Oh
Caterina Valsamakis
Martyn Wiltshire

Special thanks to:
Cedric Price
The Marchioness of
 Dufferin and Ava
Peter Langan
John Prizeman

1984–85

Unit Master
Peter Wilson

Technical Tutor
Andrew Walker

Tutor
Neil Porter

Visiting Critic
Professor Lars Lerup

Students
Zehan Albakri
David Boe
Byron Carlson
Gabrielle Church
Costas Davaris
Nilus de Matran
Andrew Kamins
Scott Kemp
Katrin Lahusen
Annabel Lahz
Richard Lundquist
Iliona Outram
Alberto Rivera
Michael Seroff
Ban Shubber
Tanagra Soares
Martyn Wiltshire
Sejal Patel
Argi Skroubelou

Special thanks to:
John Hejduk
Cedric Price
The Marquis and Marchioness
 of Dufferin and Ava
Joanna Drucker
Peter Davidson

CORNEL NAF

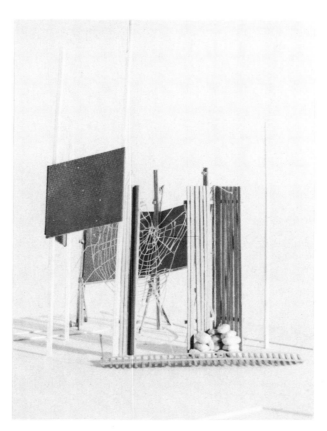

spider house

hunting ground

PROJECTS

CORNEL NAF

WILLIAM FIREBRACE

HIDEHIKO ASANO

HENRY ALDRIDGE

NEIL PORTER

GUY COMELY

RICHARD LUNDQUIST

BAN SHUBBER

MICHAEL SEROFF

MARTYN WILTSHIRE

LOUIS RICO GOODWIN

KATRIN LAHUSEN

CORNEL NAF

The polemical aspect of the Spider House is not a theoretical manifesto, nor is it to do with dexterity of reference. It is to do with the process of designing itself. Extrapolated, this process becomes a journey, a subjective evolution in which programme, site and subject repeatedly mutate. Naf scribbles for months, an obsessive process whose calligraphic product is at once casual and precious. His final product is precise, a self-generated building.

The Spider House evolved in three identifiable phases. First the given programme for a journalist's house in the Fleet Street district of London. The journalist as fashion writer and interviewer of 'Great Designers of Italy' becomes metaphorically and then literally the spider, trapping her victims in webs of appearance. A protracted phase of spider research and spider-like drawings produced an architectural vocabulary for the London site. Wooden screens; aesthetic insulation to isolate the hunting ground from its context; webs and food bags; a typewriter of course; and an overall impression of decomposition.

In the second phase the subject becomes 'architectural fashion', specifically Libera's much-revered Villa Malaparte on Capri – this is the spider's prey. More elements of the architectural vocabulary emerge as the house is eroded in another extended series of drawings. Only the famous pink wall remains. As with all spiders' food, decomposed elements are bound and hung by webs. Further platforms and planes become necessary for their storage. Finally, even Capri is consumed by the spider's stratagem.

The annual meeting of Italy's twelve top designers (Armani, Versace, etc.) on Capri provides the programmatic content for the third stage, 'The Spider House as Fashion Institute'. This is a set of monumental artificial islands walls standing in the Mediterranean. From the spider's journey and his encyclopaedia of sketches, Naf now produces a highly specific set of drawings. A language of construction emerges that looks superficially familiar, but on closer inspection proves to be highly idiosyncratic and inventive. The obvious influence of a surrealist critique in this play with convention is even more striking in the final technical drawings. Here are boat arrivals, cells for designers and catwalks for models, a most extraordinary building specified in the most deadpan detail.

Such a process is by definition indulgent, but as we are now outside the canons of modernism, such avenues are necessary research, especially when connections are made between personal, architectural and popular myth.

decomposition of the villa malaparte

decomposition of capri

institute wall with designers' cells

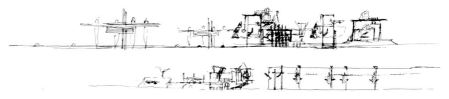

capri and the island of fashion

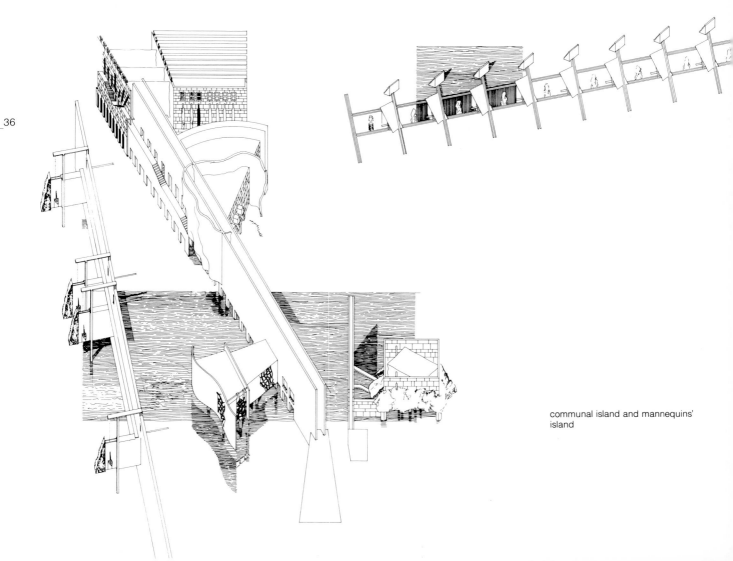

communal island and mannequins'
island

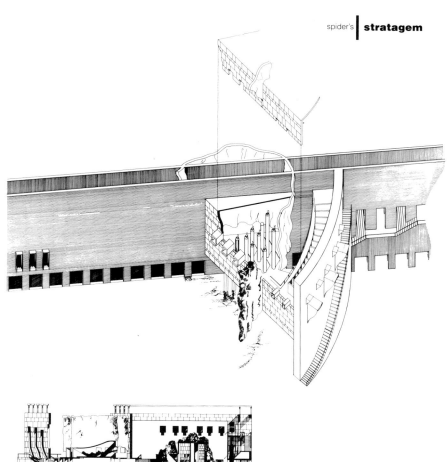

theatre with columns of fame

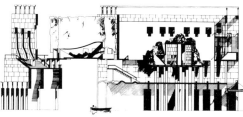

island of toilets

communal island elevation

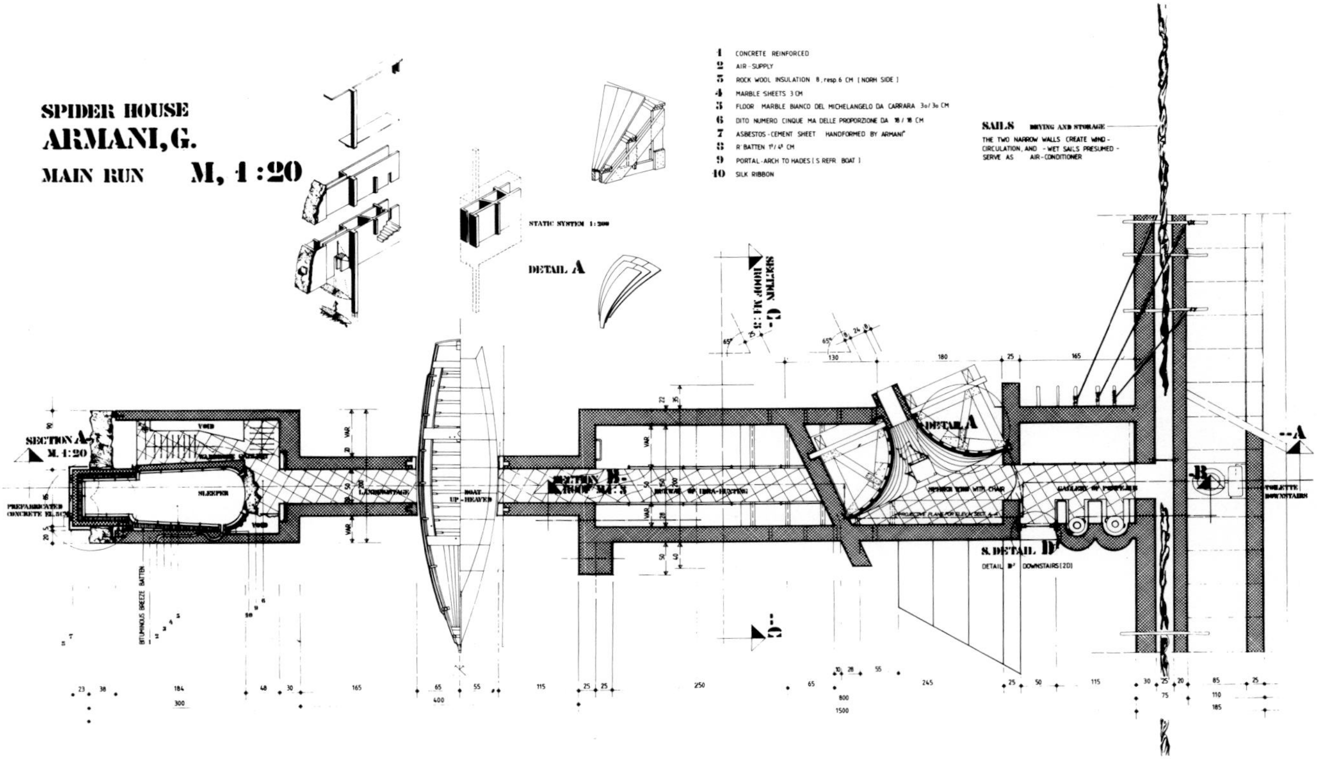

SPIDER HOUSE
ARMANI, G.
MAIN RUN   M, 4 : 20

1   CONCRETE REINFORCED
2   AIR - SUPPLY
3   ROCK WOOL INSULATION 8, resp 6 CM (NORH SIDE)
4   MARBLE SHEETS 3 CM
5   FLOOR MARBLE BIANCO DEL MICHELANGELO DA CARRARA 3o/3o CM
6   DITO NUMERO CINQUE MA DELLE PROPORZIONE DA 18 / 18 CM
7   ASBESTOS - CEMENT SHEET   HANDFORMED BY ARMANI*
8   8' BATTEN 1"/ 4" CM
9   PORTAL - ARCH TO HADES (5 REPR BOAT)
10 SILK RIBBON

SAILS DRYING AND STORAGE
THE TWO NARROW WALLS CREATE WIND -
CIRCULATION, AND - WET SAILS PRESUMED -
SERVE AS   AIR-CONDITIONER

STATIC SYSTEM 1 : 200

DETAIL A

38

main run, plan of designers'
quarters

CORNEL NAF

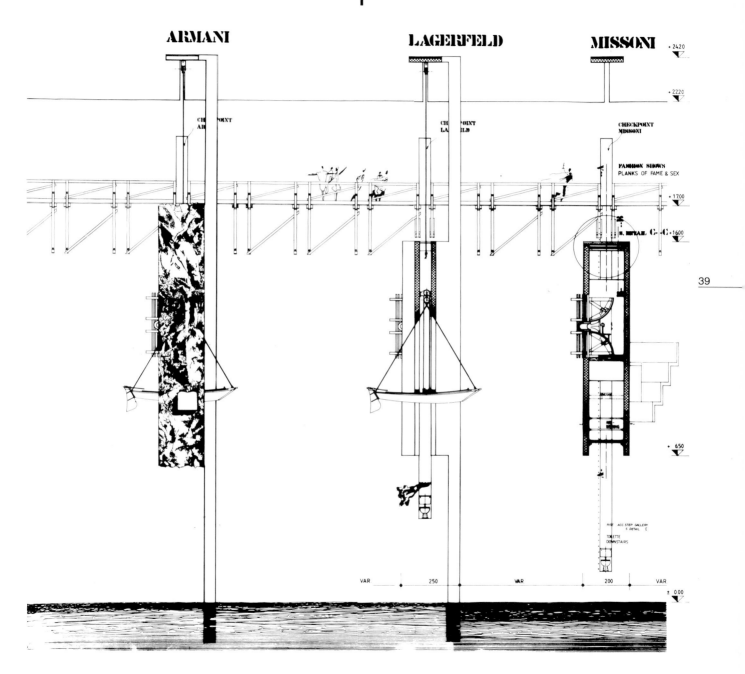

ARMANI

LAGERFELD

MISSONI

designers' quarters, section

middle floor, upper and lower illusion cones and shelf for sky domes

telescope column bedroom

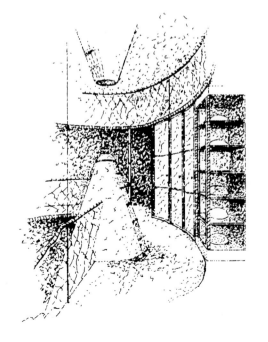

WILLIAM FIREBRACE
COLUMN/COLUMNIST/HOUSE

The house, situated on the pavement beside Holborn Viaduct, appears to change according to the relative positions of view. The two readings are that of the occupant – the writer – and of the public. To the latter, the house is apparently empty, while the columnist cohabits with the mechanisms of illusion.

The public are given access to the base, the bisecting bridge and the observation platform on top. They miss the space hidden within, which is penetrated by the two cones. The upper cone contains at its base a model of the arcade and telephone booths below. Gazing down on the gloom the column appears empty. The upward illusion works similarly, but this cone is capped with a dome matching the sky. Alternate domes are on a nearby shelf.

The house itself is accessed from a phone booth, has a bed between telescopes and a desk in the window. The writer at work is obviously at home.

PERSPECTIVE

FALSE

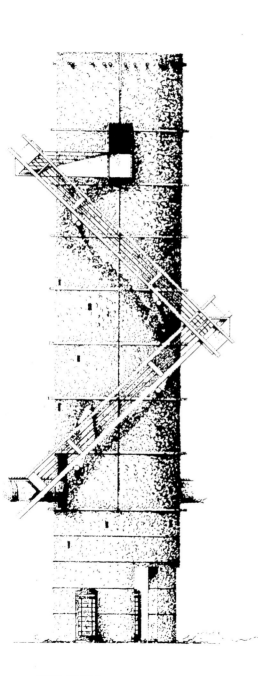

actual elevation

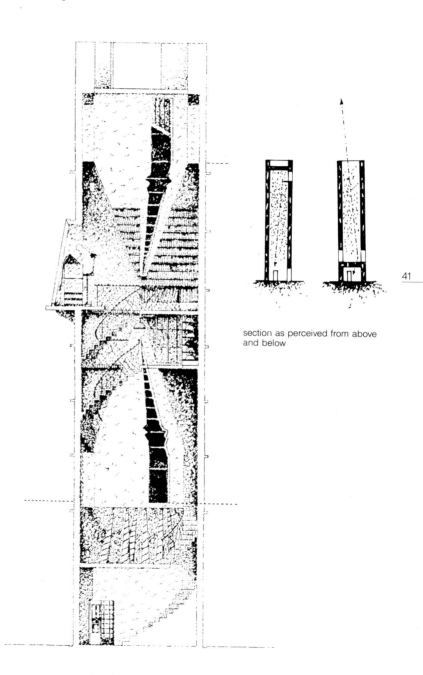

actual section

section as perceived from above
and below

41

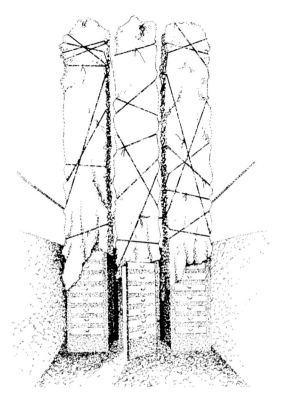

government cover-up tableau

writing rooms

WILLIAM FIREBRACE
PRESS ARCHIVES

Two buildings identical in shape and volume face one another across Fleet Street. The first, hidden maze-like, contains the memories of newspaper stories; the second, exposed and orderly, provides accommodation for nine writers producing continuing versions of the same stories. The standard stories are:
– Drugs Haul
– Royal Occasion
– Terrorist Atrocity
– Bizarre Sexual Confessions
– Government Cover-Up
– Faithful Pet Saves Family
– Pensioner's Pools Win
– African Coup
– Football Fans Rampage
The buried building is a stationery shop, selling pens and blank paper. The stories are here manifested as iconic tableaux (shelving systems), architectural memory aids. The other building is a café with writing rooms above and tickertapes and paper being printed on with current versions of the nine stories.

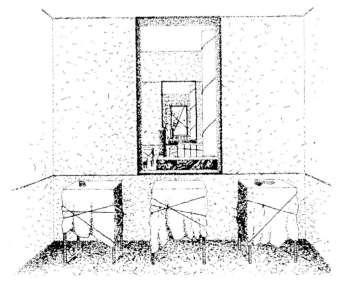

site plan: the two buildings

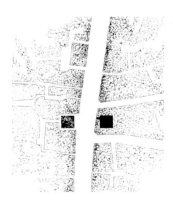

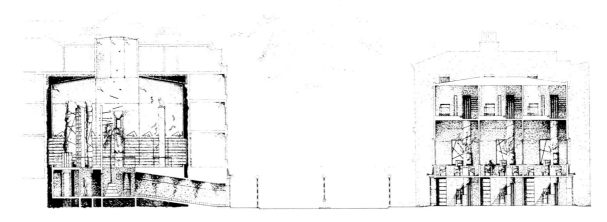

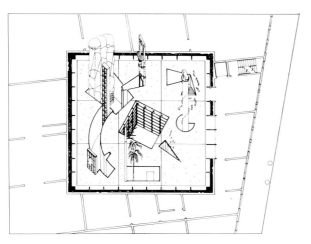

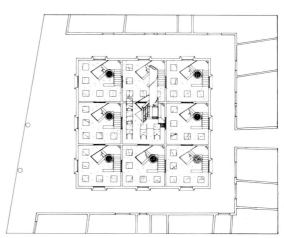

1 section across fleet street

2 plan across fleet street

3 elevation of exposed building

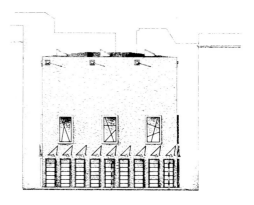

HIDEHIKO ASANO
LIGHT HOUSE/DARK VILLA

The programme was for an urban villa on a 20x20m section of a disused railway viaduct and an associated station of service. The service is a lighthouse focusing a single beam on the villa. The villa consists of architectonic, metaphoric and figurative layers around its centre. It is an asylum, a mechanism for architectural shock therapy for the single occupant held at its centre.

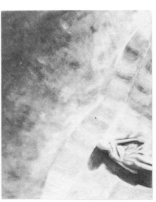

mode of occupation

axonometric: the beam

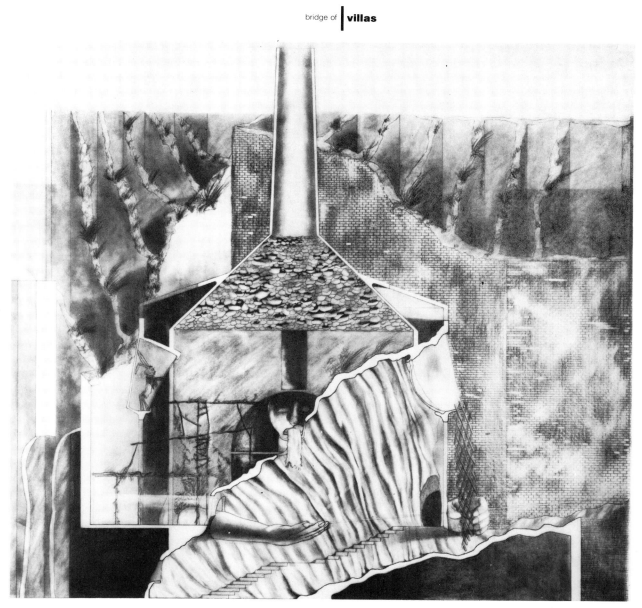

dark villa, section

HIDEHIKO ASANO
BORDER CROSSING

From the original hypermarket and border brief, a complex metaphoric language is developed. The resulting architectural figures push the descriptive capacity of formal syntax well beyond the realms of convention. The sensibility is a critical one, influenced strongly by the writings of Yukio Mishima. The subject is that of contemporary experience, morality and amorality. Functional components from the original programme metamorphose into four figurative states (both subject and object): the traveller, the border, the city, the way out.

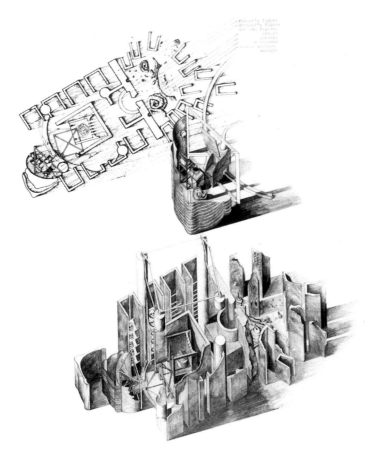

1 THE TRAVELLER... herself a late twentieth-century hut, an environmentally influenced figure. Her own figure, four columns, a sophistication machine for choosing masks for the appropriate situation. Translation machine, emotion becomes sophisticated words, odour is removed by water.
– Mother's figure, a large piece of furniture
– Father's figure, a bookcase (the brain) containing among others the words of Kafka, Genet, Poe and Mishima.
– Brother's figure, a pyramidal gold frame (domestic valuables).
– Lover's figure, a concrete wall with fireplace burning incense which fails to negate aphrodisiac smells.
– Friend's figure, a store room for masks.
The traveller is still in her adolesence.

2 BORDER CROSSING... more than half the border is a decoy, to waste the traveller's energy; the rest is clues leading to the real border.
– The mystified entrances, in series with mannequin officers, a souvenir shop, a tea room.
– The labyrinth, a further waste of energy, but with a picture of the actual entrance.
– Signs to the real border; clues. A frame, a model of the actual border, a fixed weathercock.

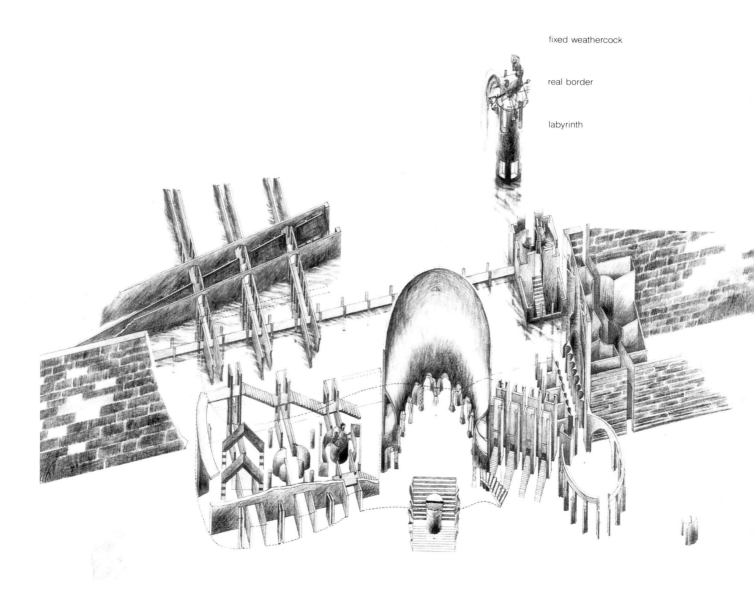

fixed weathercock

real border

labyrinth

pretend border

second mystified border with tea room

model of real border

48

city beyond the border

hilarious palace of suicide

3 THE CITY... she, the hut, has grown up into a city by utilising people's figures. Her mask collection grows, her sophistication grows, she has lost her genuine face. If sophistication is self-estrangement, then meaninglessness has been achieved through seductions.
– Head, none, only remotely controlled masks.
– Body, an empty garden surrounded by the Prison (power), the Library (knowledge), the Amphitheatre (fame). Near the centre are Hospital, Mortuary, Abattoir, Crematorium and Cemetery. Beyond this are three further elements – the Valley of Carnal Desires, the Alley of Rhetoricists' Brothels and the Exhibition of Strategically Manipulated Works.

4 EXITS FROM THE CITY... there are two ways to escape:
– Via the Hilarious Palace of Suicide. Here people throw away their masks and, using petrol, burn themselves. As soon as the body is burned water puts the fire out.
– Via the Endless Chain of Meals. This repetition of meals and bowel evacuation is articulated by ritual or prosaic dining room and toilet cells. Each cell has two columns, wedged columns for each dining room, linked columns for each toilet. These two types alternate in series. A precise weight of feces is required to unlock the door to the dining room. People are free to get out but they will always be aware of the omnipresence of the Endless Chain of Meals.

HIDEHIKO ASANO

endless chain of meals

everyday working life

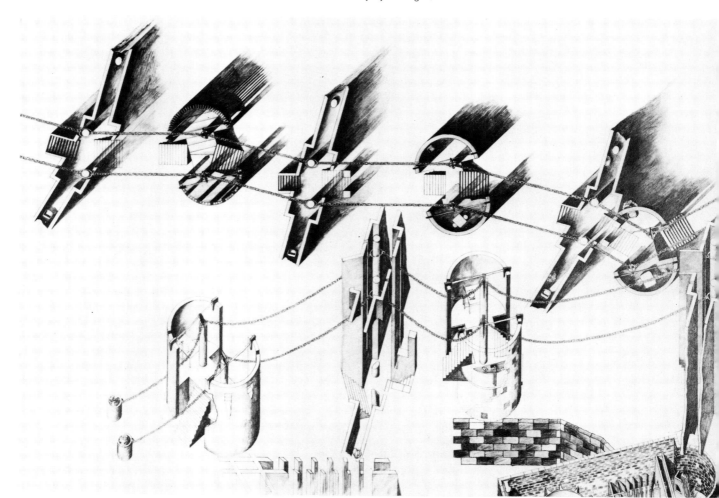

1 upstream elevation

2 front elevation

3 downstream elevation

4 elevation with blackfriars bridge

5 section

50

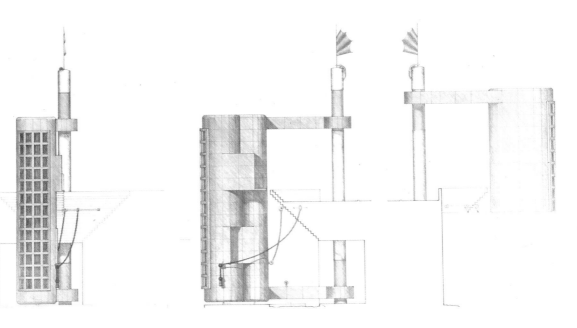

1

2

3

4

plans rotating with tidal changes

HENRY ALDRIDGE
COLUMN/COLUMNIST/HOUSE

One of sixteen markers of the perimeter of the press precinct. Given site: Thames Embankment between Blackfriars rail and road bridges.

DENSIFICATION

A tactic to promote Architectural Invention by inserting even more elements in an already congested piece of the city.

Column House: a stack of 'minimum' rooms (minimum = enough room to swing a cat = radius 1.5m). Add stairwell for compound column. Set at the end of a long and narrow canyon, the building refutes the axiality of its site by moving, rudder-like, from side to side with the changing tides. It also moves vertically, Thames maximum tidal rise 7m, house draught 5m. As register of natural forces, the poetic of the house is precisely materialised, a tough, controlled object.

51

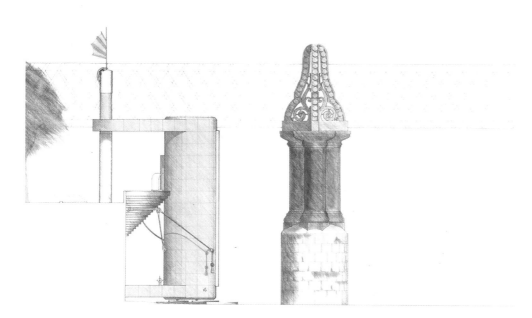

site, the urban canyon

5

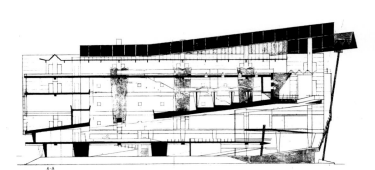

cross section

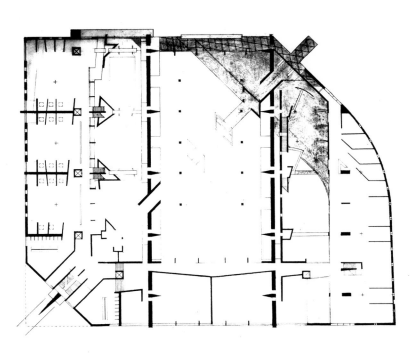

lower plan

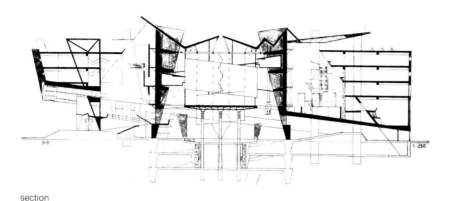

section

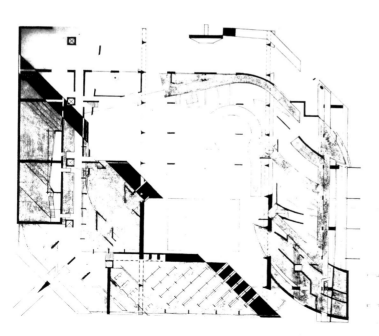

upper plan

NEIL PORTER

BBC HEADQUARTERS – AN IMAGE FOR SOUND

The building fills an entire block and responds to the complex transition from Regent Street to Portland Place, a typical London hiccough in the urban pattern.

The tripartite division of the building is generated by absorbing external forces. The axis of Portland Place enters the large central hall and is held by the two solid side blocks.

The subject is movement, a building densely and intensely occupied. From Regent Street the public filters in and under the working spaces, marshalled movement. The principal working grain of the building is in the opposite direction, an ascending datum which rises diagonally through all the principal spaces (newsroom, sound archive and ramps across the central technical void). This activated movement plane is towards, and thus defines, the relationship with the existing 1930s BBC building.

53

DENSIFICATION

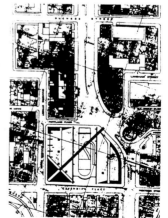

site plan

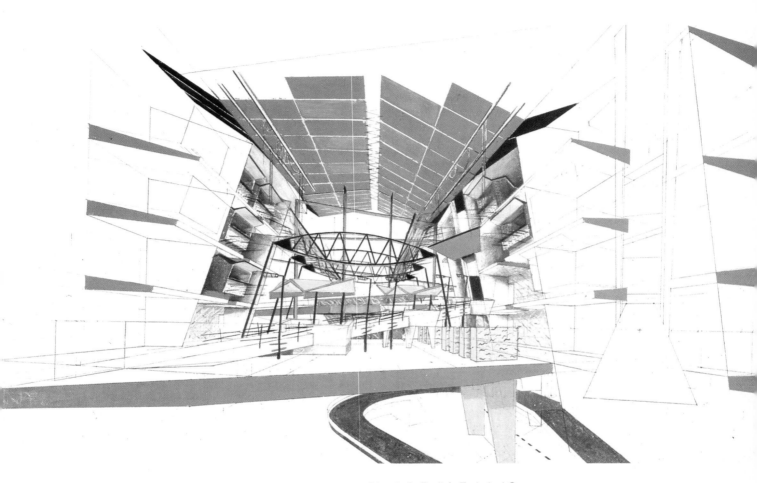

PERSPECTIVE

INTERIOR

Left: Radio's Technical Canyon divides the building. A central void, the space of sound. Walls are lined with clip-on recording rooms, up-datable technology.

Right: Radio's Public Image: a block, an articulated corner. The public filter in from Regent Street, the canopy concludes the Portland Place axis.

NEIL PORTER

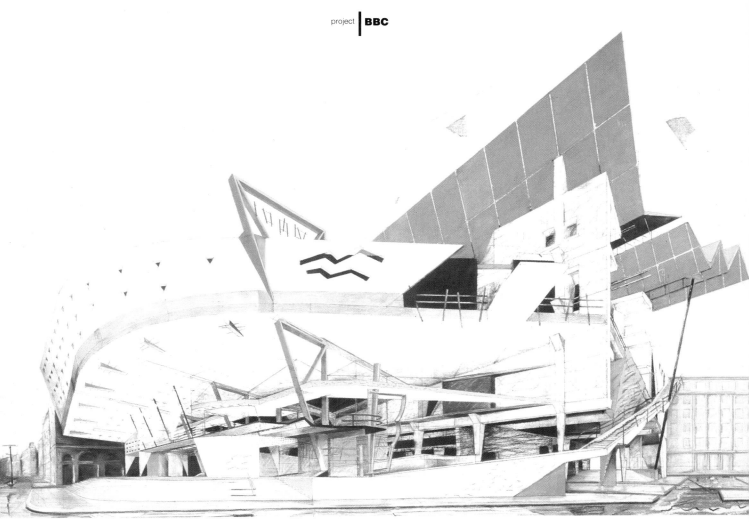

PERSPECTIVE

BLOCK

GUY COMELY
LANGAN'S RESTAURANT

To place one building on top of another implies an intense, layered urban condition. Such densification was implicit in the brief for a restaurant sited above, but not touching, an electrical substation located in the labyrinth of London's West End. From this point an intuitive leap was made, the building was drawn naively (a naivety obviously informed by contemporary painting): it is a horse. An unlikely model, but with its four legs set firmly on the ground it presents an obvious structural solution to a tricky problem. It also conveniently locates the other element of the brief, the house of the restauranteur, as the 'rider'. Copious reworkings refine anatomical hierarchies, legs as essays in the loadbearing character of steel and concrete, and a massive backbone beam to span the length of the entire structure. From the beam is hung the rib-like cage of the dining chamber. The shed-like quality of this space is set against a more articulated head and tail, service and entry points. The rider becomes wooden hut, an aerial retreat.

opposite: dining chamber

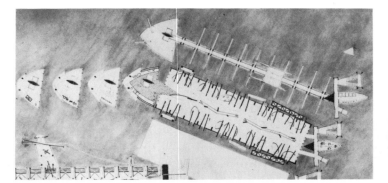

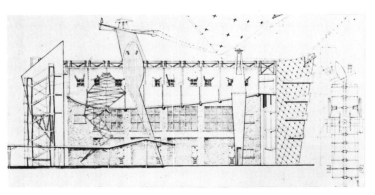

elevation showing structural legs

STRUCTURAL **FIGURATION**

The pitfall of confusing the product of the architect with the fundamentally different product of the painter is at this stage avoided by a switch in the *modus operandi*. Drawings become precise, measured and ultimately disciplined by the rationale of perspective, man-centred at the apex of the optical cone. Now the optical relationships are to be observed from the outside. A spider's web of geometrical trajectories connects, as in Duchamp's *Batchelors*, the various discontinuous projections of plan, elevation and three dimensions. On a single page are found multiple representations of the same object, not floating in anti-gravity, but changing in scale as they slide up and down the construction lines, and blossom into three dimensions as they traverse the 'picture plane'. Such composite perspectives are both design tool and representational technique.

This restaurant is a provocative and highly individual architecture. Constructive and material qualities take precedence over theory, the figurative generates, perspective disciplines, but it is the architectonic animal itself, its status as artefact, that finally constitutes its validity.

Figurative sketches: restaurant as horse, structurally straddling the existing substation, restauranteur as rider.

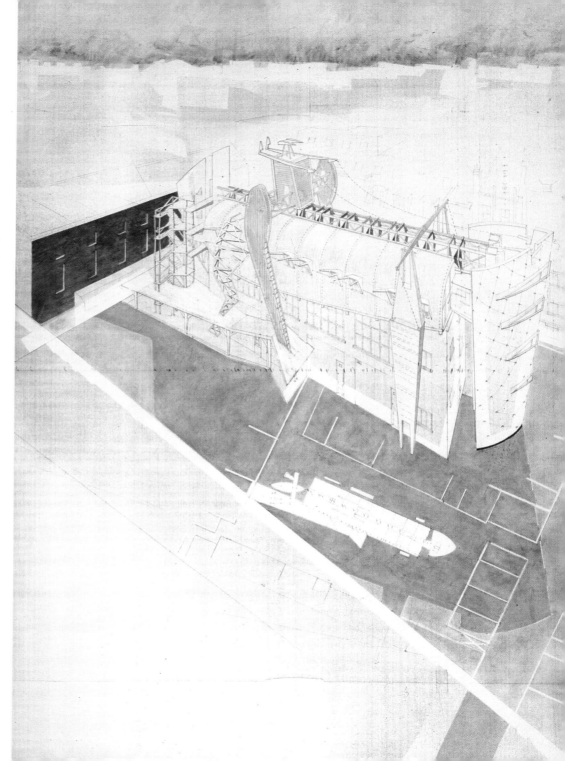

Langan's rooftop restaurant
on the London skyline.

GUY COMELY

In these projects models have taken precedence over drawings as both generative and representational technique. Such an emphasis on making, on the tactile qualities and physical presence of the object itself, signifies a profound shift in sensibility. These buildings are informed but not referential, they have their internal logic but not the rationale of convention, they are skins and frames made from materials whose link with the earth has not yet been obscured.

RICHARD LUNDQUIST

market pavilions, new covent garden: rooftop boat house

market pavilions, new covent garden: truck driver's house, to be entered by somersaulting

APPROPRIATION

Model: Langan's Restaurant as space borrowed from existing building. The parasitic architecture is one of skin and frame, a sophisticated rusticity, both figurative and tectonic.

Station **1** skyward – caged ascent.

Station **2** earthward – tidal plough.

Station **3** impossible/horizontal connections – ties.

Station **4** water/sky connections – ties.

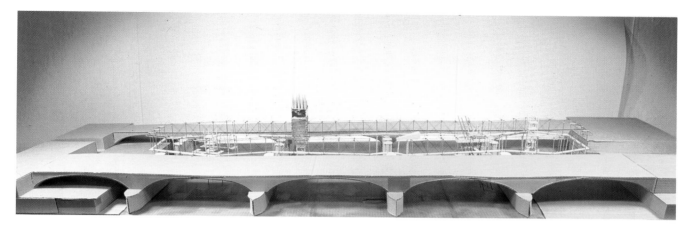

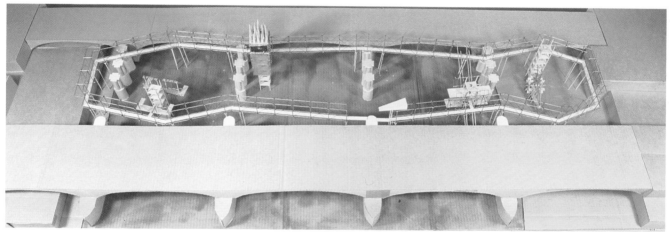

a bridge that connects only to itself

a bridge that prescribes a space

a bridge to be within not upon

a bridge to be understood through
the understanding of making

TECTONIC

A new bridge between the
existing rail and road bridges.
This exploration of
'bridgeness' is to be
understood first through the
process of making, then
through the cycle of
occupation and finally through
the prescribed contemplatory
intervals (building, dwelling,
thinking). A project concerned
with revelation rather than
rationalisation.

RICHARD LUNDQUIST

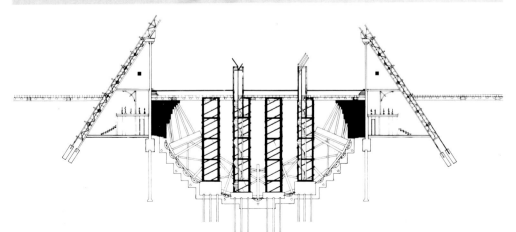

BAN SHUBBER
CLANDEBOYE ARTS INSTITUTE

The rubbish dump condition of the site is renaturised by the initial landscape treatment, an organisation into strips (steel, wood, glass, bone, etc. – a ubiquitous tidy-up). One diagonal is then developed as Linear Institute, a sequence from Gate House to Art Gallery to Residential Bridge to the Art School itself. Each piece fills out invented forms with tectonic logic, the art of architecture.

elevation

bridge of residential towers accessed from above

section

65

detail of bridge rooms in glass, steel
and timber

BAN SHUBBER

CALAIS HYPERMARKET

The programme for a
Hypermarket at the border
crossing in Calais is here
reduced to its essentials.
A string of chambers, a
method of construction
involving the casting of panels
on the surface of the dunes,
and carparks. Bunker-like
sheds take on the silhouette
of their site, an archaic and
fundamental bond between
building and earth.

Calais

long elevation, carpark, lighthouse,
customs hall and market halls

lighthouse with hypermarket halls,
imprints of the dunes

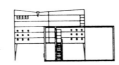

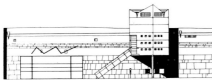 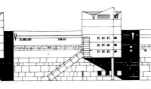

clandeboye, motel huts emerge from the wall

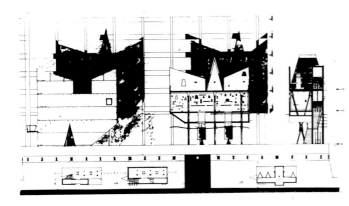

tottenham court road, huts as free-standing pavement pavilions

MICHAEL SEROFF
TYPOLOGY OF THE HUT

The theme of 'hut' is here developed in three consecutive five-year projects. The small architectural figure gradually evolves towards an autonomous status. Taking on the role of provocateur, this vagabond element becomes a sort of architectural shock therapy for ailing urban sites.

The hut first appeared as motel units penetrating the wall of the supermarket at Clandeboye. Then in Tottenham Court Road, three independent huts took on the role of freestanding facade – electronics kiosks, whose figurative character and tectonic inventiveness compensated for the architectural poverty of the office block backdrop.

The nomadic potential of the type was further developed for the final Blackfriars project. Here large huts strung pier-like across the Thames manufactured smaller huts (type becomes programme). In this Institution of the Arts the small huts are fabricated in the Hut Factory, then, equipped with their exhibition, are launched. The first venue is the Arena for Exhibition Openings at the far end of the bridge. From here they disperse, taking up their true vagabond role, travelling the streets, architectural and cultural propaganda.

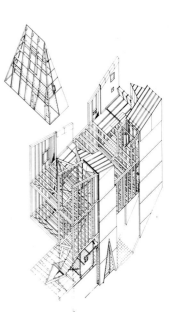

art arena

art factory

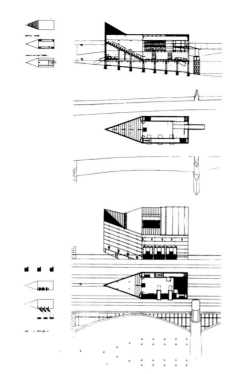

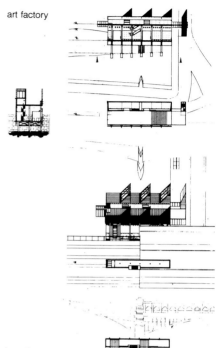

between blackfriars rail and road
bridges, the new bridge of huts; left:
the art arena; centre: the art
promenade; right: the hut factory

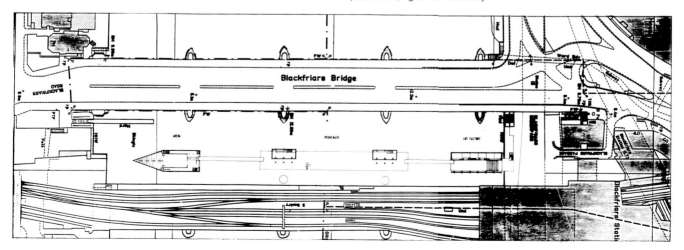

left: arena at low tide

right: art hut enters the arena

The bridge stops short of the South Bank, its public deck reaches via art hut factory and central café to the arena. Huts launched from here have the potential to lay siege to any context (infinite connections for the bridge). As vagabond architecture the hut is remedial, catalytic and provocative cultural as well as architectural propaganda.

art hut leaving factory

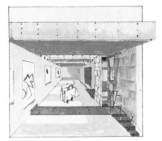

art gallery walk

arrival to factory – promenade level

Art hut production building,
a larger hut producing
travelling exhibitions, small
movable huts.

71

Art hut launching building,
a theatre for the private view,
arena for openings.

MICHAEL SEROFF

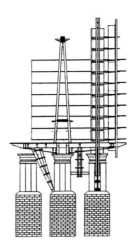

72

APPROPRIATION

PLATFORM HOTEL ON FOUND COLUMNS

MARTYN WILTSHIRE

BRIDGE 409

The new bridge building is composed of a sequence of elements bound together by the visual logic of perspective. Seen from without (an ideal viewing point at the centre of Ludgate Circus) the different pieces cohere to form a composed urban set. Each separate element has its role in this built cone of vision: the river's edge is a procenium frame, bridge hotels are stage flats and the roof of the Chair Institute is at a different scale to the apparent stage plane leading up to the artificial horizon.

Seen from within, each piece has its own subject and chair-related use. The current station concourse is reorientated and reconnected to the street (waiting seats). Towers on top of the existing columns are projected up as platform hotels and rentable chair-related rooms (dentist's etc.) on the connecting wall. A public route connects these towers and then passes through the Chair Factory and Museum before connecting to the street level on the Southbank.

While taking up contextual responsibilities and activating the site, this project also presents a complex hierarchy of structure and figuration.

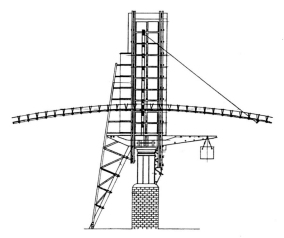

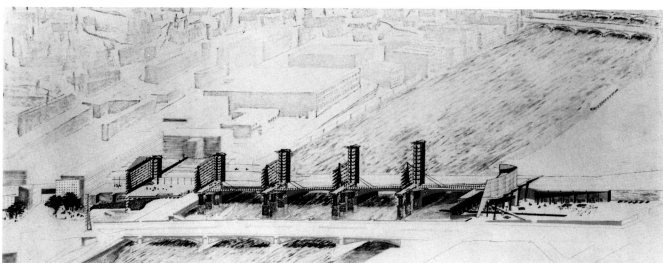

isometric towards st paul's

bridge elevation

bridge 409, perspectival additions as generated from ludgate circus

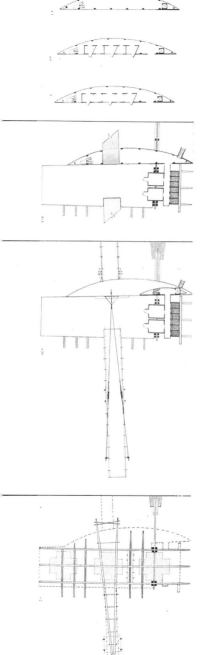

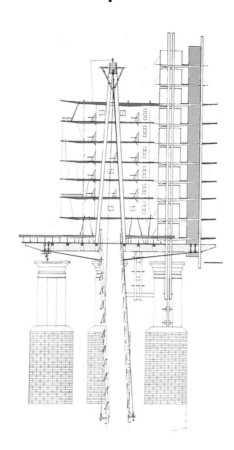

elevation to bridge 409

– existing columns

– public platform

– chair wall

– hotel wall

MARTYN WILTSHIRE

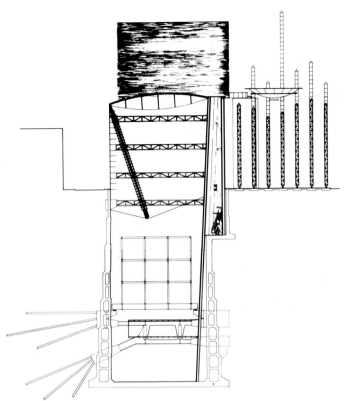

pit section, park of sound and
technical pit

LOUIS RICO GOODWIN
THE BBC

A temple of sound which
projects acoustic qualities into
the realm of visual sensation.
Minimalist graphics are a
counterpoint to the
orchestration of terrifyingly
strong spaces. The site has
four principle zones:
1 The park of sound – a
public space – each mast
topped with a horn phased to
bounce sound signals against
the wall and reflect the one
point in the park.
2 Stainless steel sound wave
wall with archive at its base.
3 Sound technical pit;
polished concrete walls;
suspended production spaces;
technical wall.
4 Pyrex glass office box.

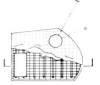

control room office floor

ground floor

entrance level

studio framework office floor,
technical wall

news room

pit bottom

pit section

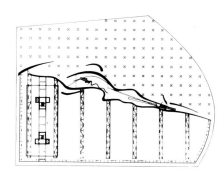

ground plan park of sound, wall pit

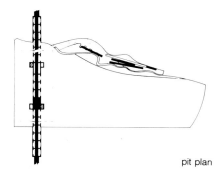

pit plan

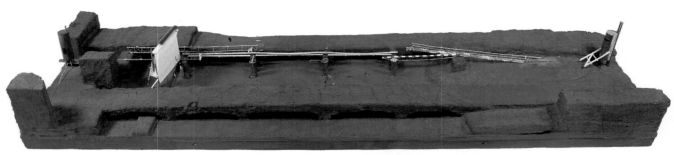

78

sited elements

floating elements

KATRIN LAHUSEN

BLUE BRIDGE

In contrast to the mass of the existing columns, delicate insertions here choreograph the tentative act of bridge crossing. Circus itself or set for circus, these icons are seen against the one city-scale object, an outdoor movie screen (the frame of the virtual). Within this blank wall, occupation, both public and private, is allowed.

APPROPRIATION

MINIMAL

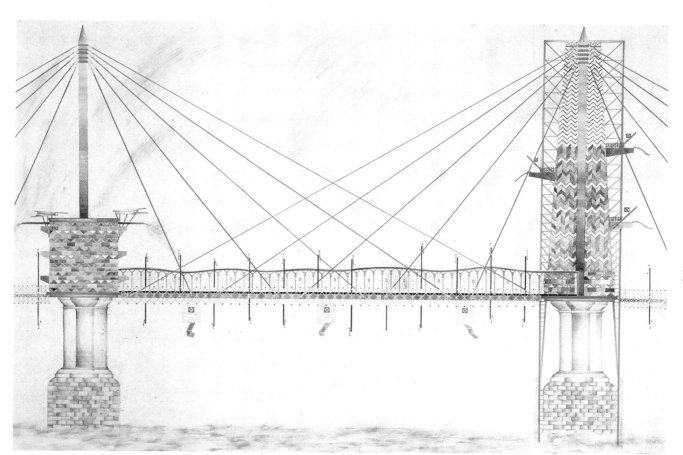

BAN SHUBBER
BRIDGE ASYLUM

APPROPRIATION

SENSUAL

The remaining columns of Cubitt's railway bridge, each with a loading capacity of 400 tons, become the isolated site... Bridge as sanctuary. The bridge as a state of disconnection from the everyday and from the city is here exaggerated. A sanctuary or asylum is both massive and delicate, decorated and tough. The vantage is crucial.

In the same series:

THEMES I: Architecture and Continuity
Introduction: Alvin Boyarsky. Introductory articles: Dalibor Vesely,
Peter Carl and Mohsen Mostafavi.
96 pages, illustrated, 6 in colour, 210x210mm
1982
Price £12.00

THEMES II: Spirit and Invention
Introductory articles: Peter Cook, Christine Hawley and Ron Herron.
96 pages, illustrated, 210x210mm
1983
Price £12.00

THEMES III: Discourse of Events
Introductory articles: Bernard Tschumi, Nigel Coates.
96 pages, illustrated, 6 in colour, 210x210mm
1983
Price £12.00

THEMES IV: People in Architecture
Introduction: Mike Gold.
60 pages, illustrated, 24 in colour, 210x210mm
1983
Price £12.00

All available from:
AA Publications, 34–36 Bedford Square, London wc1b 3es. Tel: 01-636 0974